INCIVILITIES

INCIVILITIES

Counterpath Press Denver 2010

for Lynn

BARBARA CLAIRE FREEMAN

your friend

with gratitude for
what you do for poetry!
Barbara

Counterpath Press
Denver, Colorado
www.counterpathpress.org

Printed in Canada

Library of Congress Cataloging-in-Publication Data

Freeman, Barbara Claire.
Incivilities / Barbara Claire Freeman.
p. cm.
ISBN 978-1-933996-15-8 (pbk. : alk. paper)
I. Title.
PS3606.R4453I53 2010
811'.6—dc22

2009028176

Distributed by Small Press Distribution (www.spdbooks.org)

CONTENTS

The Second Inaugural 1

Typical Morning Suffusion 2

And Stepped From the Asphalt into The Quaking Grass 4

The Hurricane of Independence 5

In the Garden Of 6

Incivilities 9

Incivilities (2) 10

Incivilities (3) 12

In the Garden of Discarded Glass 14

First Georgic 16

In the Garden of Abbreviated Violence 18

Things as They Might Have Been 20

Ghost Town in Disarray 21

Man of Gold 22

Second Georgic 24

Leapt from the Steeple into the Blood Grass 25
The Closing Bell 27
The Third Inaugural 28
Apocryphon 31
In the Garden of Disorganized Sedentary Rocks 45
When the Moon Comes Up 46
In the Garden of the Carelessly Sequenced 48
One Down, Seven to Go 50
Diminishing Returns 51
Analogy 53
Asyndeton for Lincoln 54
In the Garden of Discarded Glass (2) 55
Fernlike Patterns Appear in the Aftermath 56
Praeteritio for the Absent 57
Came a Tiger 58
The Music the Stone Makes 59
The Last Truly Foreign Country 60
No, But it Should 61
Fourth Georgic 62
General Motors 63
In the Garden of Migrating Ghosts 64
Walking Barefoot through the Panic Grass 65

Notes 67
Acknowledgments 68

For Christianna Nelson

and Sarah Margaret Stone

THE SECOND INAUGURAL

Dear Necessity, the magnitude
and difficulty of the trust to which the voice
of my country has called arises from the recent
tempest, adopted by the Spanish to name
the storms they encountered in New Times
Roman. These reflections, bracketed
by floods, have forced themselves
so strongly on my mind that I fear
Hurakan, who commands winds
from the east. In the night there is a coming
and going of people, but where are the former
ties? Although the wounds of many
of you have begun to fester,
there are none under the waters, there are
none. In this conflict all I dare aver
is that it has been my faithful study
to collect a duty from a just appreciation
of every street lamp in Philadelphia. If I
have violated willingly or silently
the injunction thereof, I may
(besides incurring constitutional punishment) be subject
to the upbraiding of all who are now
witnesses of this present solemnity. I did
not say, "In this chapter begins your future, it cannot be put out by fire."

TYPICAL MORNING SUFFUSION

A map of cracks catch the visiting sun

        patches of rain and showers unwind

scams my rogue trader ran where corporate fusion

        adheres the saltness of time the vasty deep

although silver linings could help weather

        the fund's downturn a single malt colored slice

of volatility can't outlast the arctic front or yield

        a higher ground for fog when bacteria invade

every ecological niche the market delivers

        weak growth in after-hours pipelines

run dry moonlight through unbidden

        genetic fingerprints and ancient tricks

prove the bugs themselves more difficult

        to fight (some stocks literally die from the sky)

the most prevalent infection among waterfowl

        flourishes in cold weather and breeds new forms

while bad loans tick . . .

how nice to drop fifty years in a waste basket

sleep with the windows open as if everything

was going to be right as rain drops swell

as tubercular masses or strings of beads

drenched with bottled water forgiving

the consumer's inability to spend, hoping

the vancomycin in the IV drips.

AND STEPPED FROM THE ASPHALT INTO THE QUAKING GRASS

When any branch   when any bell-shaped flower
of a family   is taken   was taken

Web to weave   one person   in agony
an empire   in agony   removed

Yet the instant   though it be nothing   joins
yet the nothing   though it be instant   expands

Through cedar   and cactus   delphinium   and thorn
this upheaved land   our analogies unlinked

THE HURRICANE OF INDEPENDENCE

Originates off Africa, carried by Gulf Streams,
followed Declarations of Helplessness,
took 4,170, damaged the Eastern seaboard
from North Carolina to Nova
Scotia, ruined fodder, wrecked ships,
razed houses, we knew, we did not know,
we were here after all, not there, came in
from the wilderness void of form in the early
months of autumn when weather is most
schizophrenic, come in she said, I'll give you shelter
from heat machines, convert tropical dark, tobacco
bred by negroes good as gold, not to obey
was the difference that would yield salvation
or revolt, the West to be erected, mine
by right of an election I could tell to none,
moving walls of water, people, come, she said,
between shattered windows, children tied to trees,
bodies of men and beasts lifted in the air, we
are not there, we did not know, drowned
in adjectives, she said, "I wanted to tell the story
of my country, how it became, what it began."

If I
could tell
the truth

about
what happens
to the marks

you leave

but won't stay
long enough

to watch
change

shape
change color

finally
fade

*

December
makes me

want
to terminate
every

unreliable
connection

*

The marks
turn into
syllables

I
stay

swollen

wait
for
words

breed
heirs

you'll
never

know

*

from your
whip

came
something

so far
from
decorous

*

I shudder
to recall

just how

I was
conceived

INCIVILITIES

Better to live like an options trader awake before the market
begins its metronymic stream and the first scattered symbols undo
the possibility of hope overlapping and circular than pretend style
is an inheritance anyone can use contrasted with the immortality
of currency (while wheat remains commodities are firm)
but disappearing will not serve to memorialize incivilities
weightless as words when you feel the Dow drop 360 points in one day
and the margin call comes close enough to make you weep ICE
moves upon the water thus appears a vast machine constructed only
to bring forth greed tortured by the sound of wind circling the street
as history returns to count the times you've failed to buy at price

INCIVILITIES (2)

Thick lines of trees bind the adjacent shore, weeds under
the surface bend downstream and on the steering blade
shaken by a narrow wind the market feels an oblique place.
Then shall they be cut: the sovereign debt, the wailer,

the whistler, the sloped yield curve, the rearing traveler,
the squally one, the wolf of the sail, the waverer, liquidity
puts, the never silent, the sawing back and forth, the house
of sands seaweeds and skerries, the hoarfrost, the frozen

mist, the amputated North and South that no partition
binds. When I feel a stock so hot no downdraft can chill it
then I know poetry's money, will we ever see emerald
green again? The shadow flutters on the windowpane

and looking down observes a derivative market deeper
than the polar sky. They say the economy is fine
but still bank stocks are thrashed, even the air is closer
to capitulation. The wind stops, grain stands still, rows

of crooked walnut trees and vines gather at the river
to await new beginnings in weather too cold for rain.
Time lost, specificity of place lost, certainty gone,
and purpose, all this and less but is there less? Then

tell me its name. Better to trust the Fed will shave
interest rates by 200 basis points than believe Brazil

has privatized negation. Your failures are no
longer sacred you said how the sky craves our daylight,

an arrangement of branches torn together, the loveliness
of shades able to speak yet unsubstantial. My purpose
here is to decline into the realities of the economy,
the lessons of capital, the broker, the insomniac,

the triple witch, haunted man, hedge fund manager,
horizon, and you have seen foreclosures rise like ether
haven't you wanted to invest in snow, the value
of your house down ten percent in one month and can

you tell the difference between redemption calls?
Greed's gone viral in someone's sentence but a stock
that clings to its fifty-two week high begs to be sold.

INCIVILITIES (3)

But I
am given

a body

runs behind
the wind

unmoving

expiation
date closer

then I would

sleep till dark
until I don't

want any more

No I will beg
for moonlight

cry for the

orphaned
noon though it

curbs me

chastizes
a morning

frailer than the

night and her
futures bound

to the sun

IN THE GARDEN OF DISCARDED GLASS

Burnt slopes. Mountains still
ablaze. Evenings you can hear the sparks

rush down. Tinderbox forests scorch
the blackened sky; the fire is

a thousand years from home. Even indoors
creosote smoke settles as though

we lived in an overpopulated camp.
The sun an orange spot in the dust. My kids

are having problems with their eyes.
Each generation destroys a ranch,

nor will it avail to build a temple. Wounded
bears wander into town and I have seen water fowl

fall mid-flight from heat. Yesterday exists as cinders,
embers take the shape of scrolls before the wind

scatters them toward a horizon that extends.
"Survivors?" Evoke the gods, cobble

sootfall. Firefighters received so many donations
of food, ice, socks, beer that they had to ask

that no more enflamed rhetoric be given.
Tonight the blaze lays in wait

like a predator. I look out the window and see
ash fall. Links to more American stories

can be found at the bottom of this page.
I despair when I hear that we would sooner run

out of wood than witches if ever we
begin a purge. In an effort to starve it, bulldozers

turn what used to be our neighborhood
into a field of margins. My uncle had to leave

his Harley, among other treasures.
In the glow, I fear the truth. Even indoors.

FIRST GEORGIC

The winds were first to whisper of this strange state, *with this letter comes a Negro*

(Tom) which I beg favour of you to sell to the Massachusetts legislature assembled

January 13, 1777: *but wher Unjustly Dragged by the hand of Cruel Power from their*

Derest Even torn from Embraces of tender Parents by beautiful law which renders

ice lighter than warmest water, bringing heat from like latitudes, the body's mission

to distribute, to palliate, and to import fresh supplies of cold *from a State of Slavery*

into the Bowels of a free & Christian Country Humbly Sheweth that rather than justice

what power needs is outcast, *in any Islands you may go to, for whatever he will*

fetch, & bring me in return for him One Hhd of best Molasses, One Ditto of best Rum,

One Barrl of Lymes—if good & Cheap. The inquietude inaugurates scars, stripes tangled limb within limb, juxtaposed as is the love of liberty with every ligament, America, nightbile

lies down. Sea lined with your owned dead. *The residue in good old Spirits. I shall*

very chearfully allow you customary Commissions on this affair. White and red

flowers meant to blossom when the hurdy-gurdy man went singing songs of love,

perceptions of legitimacy more than legitimacy *in violation of Laws of Nature*

Brough hear to Be sold Like Beast of Burthern Condemnd to Slavery for Life will

kill the outcast, thereby justify its hate, criminal organization needed to bear witness

northwest from the Straits, *beg favour to keep him handcuffd till you get to Sea, Sir,*

Yr Hble Servt., G. Washington

IN THE GARDEN OF ABBREVIATED VIOLENCE

line of white
verbs we say

thank you,
please, at day-

break we sleep
when night comes

we breathe
lines laid on rock-

crystal or
cash, we rise

and we rise
like whip-crested

waves, lick
grass in pastures

beside shepherds
unstill

beside gaping
potholes, a

nothing to
want, say please

thankyouplease
white as we dive

white lines
as we weep

Water decouples from white but the central pattern
comes right back at you. No need to worry if the low-lying
marshes collect too much rain when excess volume gathers

underneath the trade or the oil refiner's crack spreads
are priced through June. Moonlight passing
through glass takes on the color of glass, unstressed vowels

surround the thickness of glaciers as they drip: imagine
floating on a giant ice shelf that breaks apart and melts
moving out over the ocean and into the sea . . .

Although systems made from mobile parts are bound
to fail, it's not always easy to tell thought
from looking out a window: the grass which ought

to turn green remains bright gray—but some colors
are more equal than others where nothing gives better
than living by a river and the only boat left is a raft.

GHOST TOWN IN DISARRAY

This camp of magnificent shadows lacks
just inhabitants, nightly hauntings, public
beatings to carry out intelligent acts. You
could be thinking about October, phantoms
who sometimes live here, the air above (but
not too high), thoroughfares, ornaments
in complex and undulant braids,
holes sixty feet deep mined fluently in hope
of smoking out Old Golds or Lucky Strikes.
You thought it would all melt,
that no object could support the likeness
of such lifeless things. In Corpse Town
this power was called "mind,"
already excavated, and gold spoke.
You found its flakes in dirt
while digging a friend's grave.

MAN OF GOLD

Then money began to come to me like rivers flowing in the sun.
The Indians named me "Boy Earth Talks To" because she tells
me where the colors are, how to claim them. Always my thoughts
turned to mountains and mines. I wanted the spot of fire in metal

where dazzle yields and the vein changes shape. Remember about
mountains, what they are is not what made them. I didn't leave
St. Clair to modify metal with a sheath knife or stand
in yellow mud shoveling dirt into a cradle. "Hyrst," a thicket

of trees or forest of leaves we must resist all night, but I am not
a man of soil. My ideas led naturally to mining North America,
white as any cloud. No real enjambment followed the jets of water
aimed against the mountain to flush out minerals by their nature

barely perceived. In Poverty Hill, You Bet, Murderer's Bar, Last
Chance, on the banks of Cherry Creek or the Moreno fields, you
could hear the strange echo the rock sent back when water ripped.
It was the gold that groaned within the caving slide of gravel

stripped by hypostatization to hills, sand, sagebrush, grammar.
In parcels tied together by chance bonds, folded structures, fracture
systems. For gold was in the West and I was made of gold
and so by easy slope as if there were no thought where first

the soaring had begun it was an even brighter West: the gold came
not from what I mined but who I am. "We cannot help but admire

the man, who with indomitable and irrepressable energy, breasting
the wave of conditions, grows to become the concentration

of power and worth"; thus rising rhetoric equivalent to ruby
glass celebrated the founding ideology of the self-made man.
Was it possible to be American and not dream this dream?
In Deception Valley, Destruction Flat, Possibility Found

or Lost, I survived the fact that thing and language might lie
down together as near as words can come to earth, almost successfully
became The Man Earth Talks To, the rest of what she said unwritten.

SECOND GEORGIC

Plant Cypress in the room of all dead
        paper in proper time this Fall as I Mean
                to have groves range in a line at the South East
corner extending toward the Smoak House. Water
        is nature's slave to be planted without regularity
                at the North end, of locusts altogether & at the South,
of all the clever kind of Trees (especially flowering
        ones) that can be got, such as Crab apple,
                Poplar, Dogwood, Sasafras, Lawrel, and the Willow
in tears, our hurricane season simultaneously
        with your monsoon to be interspersed
                northward and southward at the meridian across the path
of trade limbs. It is the past not the future that interests us
        behind shuttered widows twisted winds in magnolia,
                the littler branches painted white. You said, "Elocutio,
consolatio. A brood of thirty thunderstorms circling my dear Republic's child."

LEAPT FROM THE STEEPLE INTO THE BLOOD GRASS

Had a fine trope but couldn't use it   my proper traffic with the earth
    a Mandan named Wounded Face   said to survive winter here

learn to steal numbers and live in rocks   found it a den
    of rattle snakes   landed at the Inscription   One Eye said

his ears would always be open to the dream of an easy water route across
    the Bitterroots   all night the air condensed repetition   this myth

will linger for centuries before it is   uninterrupted
    insomnia   saw swans and wild geese flying across the inky Dakotas

through dialects so thick ours could not hear them   a territory made up
    of objects connected unhappily needs figuring out all over again how to

begin in their parts   at 487 pages read ten daily should soon

reach the source   the horse found near the Kansas river

embraced the taste and mood of the water in the holes under leaves

THE CLOSING BELL

The screen was overcast and in the endless iterations
of the same type we could see no passage. The frozen

mud lying ahead paralyzed the turnpike after night
frost extended January across beautiful adaptations

that never grew as tall as we hoped. While recession
looms the branches that come and go bring to a head

the entire credit collapse, the lacework of tender offers—
ticks between options waiting like an ostrich for the strike.

You wondered if it had begun to snow, if the energy markets
might offer a safe haven. Not a shade in the house.

Parabolic moves leave the moist adhesive thing untouched;
when panic breaks exploit the swoon, stay long of the vultures

but not long of the meat. Perhaps it's too late to believe
the sins of excess liquid can be solved with more liquidity,

that the river mimics a sky. This, friend, is the life
we inherited; if not for the weather we could not hear

the wind. Clots of ice line corrugated streams, rivulets
of meltdown as the crisis unfolds: the ripple-effect, the drop,

the annihilation, the expense of feeding the dairy cows, buying
and selling, today rain, tomorrow rain, the rest is conversation.

THE THIRD INAUGURAL

Her wounded fingers, her dripping pen, taught me to tighten a sentence
till it begs to be absorbed in water,
extreme pleasure,
when poison crosses the limit it turns to remedy.
Throughout our history
creatures of the sea gather as fuel the silvered air
that drives their
immense engines,
and attack. Summoned by your call, whose stammar
I can never hear
without remembering a tribe of branches executed by the auburn nights:

you will join me, I trust, in believing that there are no proceedings
under which a new
government can more auspiciously commence.
Far off at sea

the winds breed. Father,

were there crimes in a storm in the storm we knew

repetitions which adorn

characters selected to devour and adapt?

In heat your august voice and all the victim's. Father,

when will the rains begin?

APOCRYPHON

X 1, 1–68, 18

You asked that I send the secret
book to a post office box near the airport.
I am not certain you will be
able to open this attachment or if
our platforms are compatible, but I
could not gainsay you. I have translated
this into the obscure language we
learned at the camp that has neither vowels
nor consonants so you will be
the lone interlocutor. Remember, beloved:
the book was given to me
under circumstances known only
to you. It is like an ear
of grain printed in many colors. The earth
is yours to scan. Train only those
who were never given names.

I 16, 31–34, 34

Shut up in a house of fire

bound with toxic [. . .] lying [. . .] chanting [. . .]

N33–

Then in [. . .] faith [. . .]. And you said “[. . .] able

to be saved?” You [. . .] intel reports. What is

4AA

called “The [. . .] unbegotten,” because you [. . .] down

10:06 a.m.

93

The [. . .] created man. [. . . men] listed

[. . .] as destroyed

III 120, 1–147, 23

Terror did not come into the world naked,
but in carry-on bags and tropes. Nothing covered
will remain; life is water, not stone. Low means
green, blue guarded, elevated yellow, orange high,
severe white. Dry, papery leaves cannot
absorb the risk of colors; a stone tablet is more
reliable than a hard drive. It is possible the compiler
disjointed what were once whole paragraphs, burying
pieces in various bodies. Stones have traces,
not origins. Beware of solvents, counterfeit spirits,
the fragrance of honey. The book is hidden in the
book, where you will find me.

VI 1, 1–12, 22

        Oxytones exist among the vowels,

diphthongs subordinate. Sounds of the [semi-

vowels] are superior to [square brackets

indicate lacuna]

voiceless consonants. Any file stored more

        than eight years is doomed: back

up or die. Consonants crowd the vowels;

they are commanded, and they submit. They

constitute

the nomenclature of the [virtual *jihad*

        cannot be divided] angels.

Consonants surrender to the [hidden

gods] by means of beat, pitch, silence,

impulse.

Summon the separations <by> a mark

and a point. A number in bold type

indicates a new page; small strokes, line

divisions; V-shaped brackets signify [. . .]

9 great

thunder. Seven megabytes of storage

equal the shadow of Alexandria.

VI 13, 1–21, 32

Shadows defective because
they take their form from
what they copy. The air
around the crypt is air,
the earth around the root
is earth. The fire around
the esplanade waits, the
water around the detonator,
water. If you fax, attach,
or photograph this text
without permission from
the unbegotten one who hides
in silence you will be
its replica.

I 43, 25–50, 18

I hesitate to print, but if it crashes so too
the archive. Old data orphaned. Type the words
on steles of turquoise, carve his name
on the azure tablet, upon the form of wax impress
an emerald likeness, and set them in the sanctuary.
Avert catastrophic system failures when the sun
is in Virgo at zero degrees and unearly summer
shines. Promise to write a promise in a script
that cannot be deciphered lest those who read
reject their fate. Signs are never symbols, save in flight.

VII 1, 1–49, 9

        The present is divided
into years into seasons
        into months into days
into syllables, as roots
        spread beneath trees,
as a body is divided by
        explosives. He alone
is undivided. Division
        takes place in Wordstar
or DeScribe, but brackets
        cannot divide the word.
We, too, are one.

II 51, 29–86, 19

Their luxury is deception. Their trees
are godless. Their souls, facsimiles. Their fruit,
poison. Their calls for amnesty, lies.
Their sleeper cells metastasize

in darkness, their place
of rest. Installing trace detection portals
is part of the pattern. Burying alphabets
in the sky is part of the pattern. Waiting

until better shadows are available is
part of the pattern. There are no accidents,
no portents. Crushing percocet and apples
is part of the pattern. Let birds

fall where they may.

VIII 132, 10–140, 27

Face to face tongue broken sleepless

bound with silence [. . .] hanging [. . .] trembling [. . .]

N33—

hunts me down [. . .]. And you said "[. . .] find

the black sea?" Solar flare [. . .] among ghosts. You

4AA

far from me when [I am] [. . .] near you [. . .] unkind

11:59 p.m.

93

Paler [. . .] than dry grass when September

[. . .] underground

V 17, 19–24, 9

He whose names are invisible symbols
is unbegotten, unbegun. Whoever has a name is the
creation of another, like those who shoot their arrows
after dark. Everyone born at the facility (pages
11 and 777 are missing, replaced with corresponding
sections from the 175 codex [no. 365]) will perish
at the facility. Simple numbers weaken the resolve
of our allies, moonlight morphs and spreads
into the pattern catastrophe management attempts
to avert. The magnetic charges weaken, corrupt,
and finally erase all data, but hidden
is the perfect day.

EPILOGUE: THE DESERT HAS TWELVE THINGS

Close the book to re-enter the book. Beware
of wells; they are not always deep. Inter
the bones between the word. Seek
a single letter, clear as frost in the long
grass. Within the brightness of a page,
the black of days. Enter the well whose sign
the center was: a scripture that obtains
only if God is a stranger from Himself.
The leaves of the book
float face down.

IN THE GARDEN OF DISORGANIZED SEDENTARY ROCKS

except
in dreams
you

can't
escape
sleep

if it
comes
will want

to eat
your limbs
pretend to

be black
horns, a
cherry

tree, in
flower
felled

Dear Sufficiency, perhaps you'll lose your best friend, partner, apartment
Maybe the power grid fails—plant, quadruped, bird, sea, earth, air, sound
And under pain, pleasure. Maybe juice dripping from a vein will not occur
Injured, alone, once you were afraid, now you know: within presence

Epic lies. Salt and basalt, tree and lichen, ape, sea lion, bird, reptile
Fifteen million purchased Louisiana in the full tide of successful experiment
Now capable of unlimited expansion from Canada's border to the mouth
Of the Mississippi, from the Great River to Shining Mountains almost

Oregon, from Missouri to states now called Abandoned, overnight
We doubled, airports closed. To scythe, regret, abolish, refuse
The right to sleep, your sadness to things indifferent seems
Abominable or necessary, being neither, as trees or sheep to night walkers

Have improper shape. Tumults re-elect Jefferson. Master, I'll be plain.
My poems can be found in recent or forthcoming editions of the 15,000
Volumes loaded at Monticello, the largest in America, hand-collected
With ammunition. What farmer, what mechanic, what laborer ever sees

A tax-gatherer? Most citizens know oranges squeezed through mesh are best
Grown in clay, lime, gravel, or granite, deceptively fair weather given
The devastating rumors, part moonlit treachery, part grace calls saline
Into the West. Dear Captain Lewis, dear Lieutenant Clark, even a threat

Badly made rushes like a comet into the Pacific as when there arises
A new, irregular meter. Although you could do nothing toward its begetting.

When I consider how much of your life can fall I find elegies, continual
Tempests where one foot hath overtaken another, every declension

Accompanied by leaks. Thus arrives the snow, the opal-colored days
As, irritated by no literary altercation, I read: "Here lies the Republic
Whose scheme of representation opens a different prospect, promises
A cure." John Adams. Imagine not having to apologize for the United
States. Let history decide which matters most, the weeds or the earth.

IN THE GARDEN OF THE CARELESSLY SEQUENCED

The primary line
wherever your

hand has lain

folded, pasted, torn
your anytime minutes

contrapuntal to recurring

transfers, the three-way
call, thee, thee,
and thee in

multiples of one
my constancy, your cross
borne even at the heart-

land's edge

*

Trace the figure
of a six-pointed

star, chalk on
a board with
the killed chalk-

star, a star
you might wear

round your neck

like a rope
a star you might

press while call
waiting waits

risk an asterisk

ONE DOWN, SEVEN TO GO

The disaster happens annually with someone else's hands

and often the supermarket was closed
earlier than it should have been, although looking

through the window we could see the aisles like a scene
from a sitcom in which romantic couples
lose and refind one another, vaguely.

Vegetables brought us here. In the air
that resembled a beginning and still managed
to order our days, rusty, lush, impenetrable,
you walked behind me, breathing. We forgot

the narrative was supposed to make us whole.
The main thing was to tell the story.
It's not grief but something purer

standing in the checkout line, Alka Seltzer.
It's a TV screen, blanker
than your therapist's mind.

The proof is that every November
shadow and sunlight invite us into an imagined world

and hold us there, captive, until coming to an end.

It occurred before a holiday for which his sister
purchased a bright red parka on sale.

DIMINISHING RETURNS

Nothing can defend a stock like visibility
        though it might seem a steal drill down
where uncertainty floods the market
        gold bars separate secular forms of absence
might make buying presents the right move
        as cash infusions from the Persian Gulf
inject sovereign wealth (hail Abu Dhabi)
        along the bottom of the agora not even the river
moves risk/reward ratios high enough
        for a tax upon the soul to kick
stones day after day spasms of time
        shake out names during quick rain you said
there are too many on the loose tonight
        because all men are equal sacrifice horses dogs
and slaves see how freedom as we dreamed it
        might have been drunk fast enough so sugar

doesn't stick to the bottom where grass almost

covers the bank and moss moves closer: once

there was something to gain now a pile of walnut

shells dyed madder will suffice.

ANALOGY

In the closed car you
pass through ruins.

Here and there the veiled
women still inhabit

thresholds of street-
side doors. The olive

trees like silver clouds
touch ground

but the cypresses are
black feathers.

There is nothing real
about this country after

dark, save the smell
of sage and lavender.

ASYNDETON FOR LINCOLN

That the earth shall not perish from the government
   of by and for the haunted man. *To those who really love*
the Union may I not speak? Does night exist to end
   up in a book? Instead of voting for who you want
to win, don't vote for who you want to lose, omitted
   like a comma used to splice a thing in two. The doublet
is not enough unless it breeds, what's needed to make
   a third. Whose woulds might have been yours
and were, then came total war. *Until every drop drawn*
   with the lash shall be paid by another drawn with the sword,
until a mobile army of metaphors springs up like earth
   beneath the rivets of your grave. The haunted men
don't vote until you see the whites of their eyes.

IN THE GARDEN OF DISCARDED GLASS (2)

Fires that cannot be kept from slipping

Fire that screams

"Fire" in an empty theatre

A thin fire has thirteen colors

Fire does not only work in wood

The thirteenth month has no color

Cannot be subtracted

From a body consumed by fire

Wills bequeath black lightning

Sirens sing

Across slippages that cannot be

FERNLIKE PATTERNS APPEAR IN THE AFTERMATH

Here in California we never lived
in a constellation of patches and pith

or a time when history was plausible

or things said well in song.
Old cradle, hunting gourd, bier of wolf and otter—

to the faithful, able disposition of their trust

is the credit due. This new maneuver
is less than the number of starlings today

on the shore and the banks falling in.

Miners unlike meanings can't be copied—
you promise not to, and the thing denied
comes out on top . . . *but can you be sure*
it has no auditor?
To be unable to survive a sentence
must lack replicas; the boss declares he won't introduce
evidence about the cave-in while listening
devices dropped into the bore hole yield silence—
when unstable ground leaves rescue efforts lost
to believe minefields are systems
whose rules can be mastered as if the entombed clause
and a miner were the same decreation.
Cases crave breath within the howling fields
not enough oxygen to . . . support grammar
trapped in fractured left-and right-branching
constructions hear something
that hasn't occurred in the owner's
mind—says it's alive and it's evil, a mountain
from which no bodies or plosives emerge
Isolation, one word left
underground cannot concurrently be

CAME A TIGER

Came a tiger on the back of a horse   happy
to have found work   before daybreak

When morning comes   the high clouds will move
but what frightens him most   under the asphalt
are sounds too loud to hear   this appalling trust

a kind of senseless dew   so much our markets have foreseen
I try to go back   but wherever I turn   America will not let

her children deleverage   Let us buy Chevron and hedge it
more aggressively   Let us set windmills in motion and cry aloud

THE MUSIC THE STONE MAKES

On the barge unmoored from its object one hour
and twenty-four minutes into the triathlon

a listener might also hear Litany playing
the same note across falling swap spreads

and a veiled, cloud-studded sky. The first voice
says something predictable about duets: people are angry,

people are sad, gathered on street corners trying
to kill time they want to sue Dairy King.

Yes, it's fun here in the agora—
that won't outlast the meltdown, not in this wind,

not in this tide. The second voice follows,
muted. For someone like her things are easier;

milk chocolate, now and then a little wine,
the traps and mandates that bewilder the whole town

stay in their place. Put a button on that!
In your throat pepper spray!

Syllabic cups of meaning overflow,
an aria soon to break elsewhere bells.

And dust as it covers the boardwalk spells out a then-again

this assimilated native strain insurance mostly what we needed
to deal with the whoosh and twist of things we called idiom

NO, BUT IT SHOULD

What to make of it, the way afternoon comes on and cracks
under the house await their time, pompous, rubbing up against
one another, hoping for the contractor
to show up, who does, finally, later than promised.

You've forgotten why he's here—mold,
dry rot, Dostoyevsky, the lake lying underneath,
a sea monster about to abort. The Inquisitor asks
if science makes belief in God obsolete. Yes, maybe,

but what I mean is that night existed before the sun's creation
helped push Him into hazy twilight and bourbon
is still *la belle dame* after Labor Day, with crushed ice
and lots of sugar. Clouds disperse, explode: your daughter

serves canapes, flirts with the contractor,
waves to a friend who no longer lives next door.

FOURTH GEORGIC

In the photograph the dollar bills resemble dolphins
bored with doing tricks for tourists in exchange
for snacks. Perhaps money makes us human—

"No, wait, it's not burning!" The water chant
you experienced in a past life occurs
every second Friday right here on the floor.

I don't know your risk profile, Barbara,
but here's what I've saved and it's from our absent city:
in one legend we are stone and terrible things happen

to stone. In another, the usurers have to remember
everything; debts unpunished in this world
can't be forgotten in the next. But the dolphins,

they lurk under every puddle, waiting
till the very last moment to rescue a person in need.
Who are these sea animals and what are they really buying.

GENERAL MOTORS

Walk with me to the end of the moment
Where the quarantine on mussels is lifted at midnight

Abloom with facades and empty skyscrapers
Watch bubbles in the car production cycle burst

Make sure that when you say "that's it"
Pastoral bottles fresh out of Coke will rush in

To empty the big numbers we found packed together
Have you ever met anyone who said "Yeah, I *like* to kill guppies"

Meanwhile creeping out of the crinoline pampas
Compost heaps limbs white powder and bones we fight over

Although it was more what they didn't sell than what they did
Tell me if it's time to play action pass and throw action deep

Most of the ideas we're talking about are bridges and roads
When the rain came through today it came through heavy

If now you cannot hear me it is because we are breaking up because
our borders are not secure because the iPod interferes with your pace

maker because there is no reason to worry about the past when the past
may never come because no one else will remember how damp

the page smells after the network goes offline. One day you will forget
the law of flood, you will take it back while the speaker behind the mirror

leads you further away from lines that began with first person address:
"let the forgetting begin." If now you cannot read him it is because distance

is what you lost once and now must drink. It is almost dark and the wind
off the river proves a field for knots of clumsy and impenetrable English

confronting the translator of Persian lyric poetry their stanzas having
become an abandoned house awaiting foreclosure as evidence

of the decade's debacle surfaces and if now you cannot hear me
it is because the sound of this night no one will remember no one else.

WALKING BAREFOOT THROUGH THE PANIC GRASS

Offering wild meal   in the rain-filled room
turquoise   dried grasses   to the ones who were fathers
country of the torn   the plaine style triumphed

Then sobbing she turned   back to her century
place of lost   beginnings   insecure homelands
off-white the color   her cell   their lies

East of our youth   where flags dissolve   darkness runs
river one mile wide   cries still   to all the directions
its wish   that no one   shall occupy this field

NOTES

"Asyndeton for Lincoln": the phrases in italics are from Abraham Lincoln's Inaugural Address and Gettysburg Address.

"First Georgic" takes from the letters of George Washington and from "The Massachusetts Slaves' Petition," 1777.

"Leapt from the Steeple into the Blood Grass" takes from *The Journals of Lewis and Clark.*

"Man of Gold": the quotation is from Wallace Stevens' prize-winning high school speech contest.

"Second Georgic" takes from the letters of George Washington.

"Apocryphon" takes from *The Nag Hammadi Library*; "VIII 132 . . . " uses language from William Carlos Williams' translation of Sappho's fragment 31.

"The Second Inaugural" and "The Third Inaugural" adapt language from the Inaugural Addresses of George Washington.

"When the Moon Comes Up" adapts phrases from the letters of Thomas Jefferson.

ACKNOWLEDGMENTS

Some of these poems appeared in the following magazines (some in earlier versions). Thanks to the editors of *A Public Space, Back Room Live (LifeLong Press), The Beloit Poetry Journal, The Boston Review, Calaveras, The Colorado Review, crazyhorse, Denver Quarterly, The Laurel Review, The Modern Review, New American Writing,* and *The Sycamore Review.*

Thanks to Timothy B. Donnelly, Graham Foust, Geoffrey G. O'Brien, Elizabeth Robinson, Peter Sacks, and Richard Silberg.

"Apocryphon" is for Brenda Hillman.

"In The Garden of" is for Michael André Bernstein.

"In the Garden of Migrating Ghosts" is for Ben Lerner.

"Man of Gold" is for Joshua Clover.

"Second Inaugural" and "The Hurricane of Independence" are for Reginald Shepherd.

"Typical Morning Suffusion" is for Chris Stroffolino.

BARBARA CLAIRE FREEMAN is a literary critic and professor of literature who has recently turned her full attention to writing poetry. She is the author of *The Feminine Sublime: Gender and Excess in Women's Fiction* (University of California Press, 1998, pbk. 2000), among many other works of criticism and theory. Formerly an Associate Professor of English at Harvard, she teaches creative writing for the Department of Rhetoric at the University of California, Berkeley. Her poems have appeared or are forthcoming in *A Public Space, Beloit Poetry Journal, Boston Review, Calaveras, Colorado Review, Crazyhorse, Denver Quarterly, Harvard Review, Iowa Review*, the *Laurel Review*, the *Modern Review, New American Writing, Sycamore Review* and *Parthenon West Review*. She is a recipient of the Discovery/*Boston Review* Poetry Award (2008), the Campbell Corner Poetry Prize (Sarah Lawrence College, 2007) and a Pushcart Prize nominee. She lives in Berkeley, California.

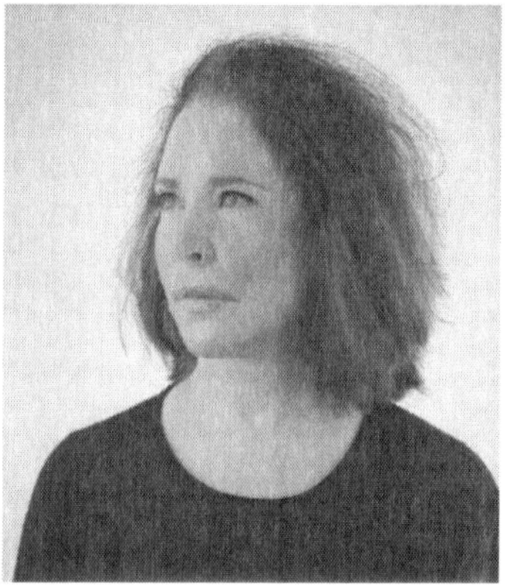